Reflections Of A Simple Ordinary Face

Mike Pouraryan

BookLeaf
Publishing

India | USA | UK

Made with ❤ on the BookLeaf Publishing Platform
www.bookleafpub.in
www.bookleafpub.com

Dedication

This is dedicated to my parents-symbols of strength & resilience

Preface

This Reflection is about celebrating life, embracing purpose, and consistently embracing the Art of the Possible.

Acknowledgements

The efforts of the Bookleaf Publishing Team in facilitating the opportunity to bring this vision of mine to life are greatly appreciated.

1. I Am

I am my Dad who came to the United States from Iran in 1954 who worked summers at Catalina Island to save up to pay for college , went on to obtain his Ph.D. at USC with a distinguished career in Business & Public Service ;

I am my Mom who sailed from Iran to the United States on the Queen Mary;

I am both my Mom and my Dad who endured and persevered in the aftermath of my Brother's Death;

I am my Aunt, who came to the United States in 1963, worked her way through School as a Seamstress while attending East Los Angeles College and Cal State LA, building a distinguished career as an Engineer, businesswoman, and public servant.

I have powered on as a proud American, proud of my hertiage and leading a life of purpose and service;

I am America

2. On Life

Life can be exciting
Life can be fun
Life can be uplifting
Life can be challenging
Life can be disappointing
Life can be profound
Life can be a window
That's why it's Life

3. Partners

Partners elevate, engage, and uplift
Partners forgive
Partners show patience consistently
Partners never give up
Partners always stand up during tough times
Partners will endure

4. Tribute to a Long Lost Brother

A Brother who was the light of the Family
A Brother who was always kind
A Brother who had a way about him
A Brother who wanted to play
A Brother who just wanted to be a child
A Brother who just withered away
A Brother who left us too soon
A Brother who watches over us
A Brother who will endure

5. Getting Old

Getting Old means An Embrace of life
Getting Old means remembering
Getting Old means appreciating
Getting Old means understanding
Getting Old means accepting
Getting Old means recognizing
Getting Old means staying graceful
Getting Old means realizing the beauty and majesty of
life

6. Divorce

Divorce is only dignity
Divorce is only about self-respect
Divorce is only about knowing yourself
Divorce is only a phase.
Divorce is only a chance to be better
Divorce is only about fairness
Divorce is only the chance to begin anew

7. Fear

There is nothing wrong with Fear
There is nothing that big a deal about Fear
To Fear is to be human
To Fear is embracing a sense of the possible
There is nothing that cannot be done without Fear

8. Being Novel

Being Novel is About Taking a Day Trip
Being Novel is About Taking an unplanned hike
Being Novel is About Exploring
Being Novel is About Embracing Poetry
Being Novel is About Embracing Chess
Being Novel is About Embracing Life

9. On Life (Cont'd)

Life is About Taking Risks
Life is About Embracing Others
Life is About Always Looking for the Good
Life is About Acting on Long-Lost Dreams
Life is About Listening to One's Heart
Life is About Daring
Life is About Smiling
Life is About Loving One's Story
Life is About Learning to embrace the adventure
Life is About Powering On.

10. The Future

The Future is About Designing a Life
The Future is About Being a Free Agent
The Future is About Embracing the Right Fit
The Future is About Being Adaptable
The Future is About Making Small Experiments
The Future is About Embracing the Present
The Future is About Flexibility
The Future is About Creating a Meaning

11. On Flying

Flying is About Dreaming
Flying is About Evolving
Flying is About Powering on
Flying is About Possibilities

12. Changing Our World

Changing Our World Requires Embracing Courage
Changing Our World Requires Embracing Empowerment
Changing Our World Requires Embracing Accountability
Changing Our World Requires Embracing Humility
Changing Our World Requires Authenticity
Changing Our World Requires Staying Hopeful

13. Focus

Focus On Learning From Failure
Focus On Celebrating Effort
Focus On Positive Self-Talk
Focus On Staying Curious
Focus On Consistency of Purpose
Focus On Reflecting
Focus On Creating the Growth Mindset

14. On Troubles

Troubles Are to be Expected
Troubles Are Part of the Adventure
Troubles Are Made to Make One Stronger
Troubles Are Made to Make One Resilient
Troubles Are Made to Build A True Sense of the Possible

15. Never Complain

Never Complain About The Challenges
Never Complain About Making Mistakes
Never Complain About What Others May Do
Never Complain About What You Can't Control
Learn to Power On For the Sake of Life

16. On Other People's Opinions

Others Are Entitled to Their Opinion
Others Are Not Entitled To Their Own Facts
Others Should be Respected for Their Opinions
It is about A Choice
The Choice is Up to Us

17. Aging

Aging Can Be Slowed if One Hydrates
Aging Can Be Slowed if One Sleeps Well
Aging Can Be Slowed if One Walks Daily
Aging Can Be Slowed if One Breathes Deeply
Aging Can Be Slowed if One Stretches Often
Aging Can Be Slowed if One Cuts Down on Sugar
Aging Can Be Slowed if One Reads Daily
Aging Can Be Slowed if One Embraces Friendship
Aging Can Be Slowed if One Eats Colorful Foods
Aging Can be Slowed if One Laughs More
Aging Can be Slowed if one Limits Screens Before Bed
Remembering, though, that Aging is Part of life
May the Aging be done Gracefully

18. The Potential For Life

The Potential For Life Must Be Embraced
The Potential For Life Is About Living The Day
The Potential For Life is About Overcoming Obstacles
The Potential For Life is About Realizing the Historical
Realities
The Potential For Life is About Embracing Justice
The Potential For Life is About Embracing Quiet
Moments
The Potential For Life is About Staying Hopeful

19. Success Is About...

Success is About Embracing Integrity
Success Is About Being approachable
Success Is About Being Collaborative
Success Is About Embracing Humor
Success Is About Embracing The Reality
Success Is About Overcoming Obstacles
Success Is About Embracing Life

20. The Future Is About...

The Future Is About Hope
The Future Is About Embracing Life
The Future Is About Recognizing What's Important
The Future Is About Being Better
The Future Is About Optimism
The Future Is About The Art of the Possible

21. A Sense of Hope

A Sense of Hope Must be Within Reach
A Sense of Hope is Always Possible
A Sense of Hope Must be Embraced
A Sense of Hope that One Must Hang On as Pain Will End
A Sense of Hope is about overcoming Pain

www.ingramcontent.com/pod-product-compliance
Lightning Source LLC
Chambersburg PA
CBHW051002030426
42339CB00007B/443